Rock, Rag, and Swing

By Teresa Domnauer

School Specialty Publishing

Text Copyright © 2006 School Specialty Publishing. Farkle McBride Character © 2000 by John Lithgow. Farkle McBride
Illustration © 2000 by C.F. Payne.

Library of Congress Cataloging-in-Publication Data is on file with the publisher.

Send all inquiries to:
School Specialty Publishing
8720 Orion Place
Columbus, OH 43240-2111

ISBN 0-7696-4234-9

1 2 3 4 5 6 7 8 9 10 PHXBK 10 09 08 07 06 05

D0111807

Hi, I'm Farkle McBride.
Join me in learning
about different kinds of music.
There are many different kinds of music.
Each has its own special sound.
Some people like folk songs that tell stories.
Some people like the rhythms of rock and roll.
There is music for dancing,
singing, celebrating, and relaxing.
No matter who you are,
there is a style of music
just for you!

Table of Contents

Early Music 4–5

Classical Music 6–7

Opera 8–9

Gospel 10–11

Ragtime 12–13

Jazz 14–15

Marching Music 16–17

The Blues 18–19

Folk Music 20–21

Country and Western 22–23

Rock and Roll 24–25

Pop Music 26–27

Rap 28–29

Thinking About It 31–32

Early Music

No one knows exactly how
music began.
It could have started with a hum
or the sound of a voice.
It could have started with clapping hands
or stamping feet.
It could have started when a person
tapped a stick on the ground
and discovered rhythm.
People made the first kinds of music
with shells, bones, sticks, logs, and stones.
They made rattles from gourds.
They sounded signals with seashells.
People made music long before
they learned to write words.

Farkle Fact

Today, in some temples in and near China, the sound of
the conch shell being blown still signals the beginning
of prayers.

Classical Music

When people think of classical
music, they most often think of
the symphony **orchestra**, the opera,
and the ballet.
Classical music began in Europe
hundreds of years ago.
At that time, most music was written
for church services.
This music was sung without
any musical instruments.
Traveling **minstrel** performers put poems to music.
They sang and played instruments.
As time passed, different kinds of music
started to grow.
The 1700s was an important time for classical music.
Composers, such as Mozart and Beethoven,
wrote famous pieces of music during this time.

Farkle Fact

Mozart learned to play the harpsichord–a piano-like
instrument–when he was four years old! He wrote his
first piece of music at age five.

7

Opera

Opera is a kind of classical music.
It began in Italy in the 1500s.
Operas are like plays, but the characters
sing instead of talk.
An orchestra plays music to **accompany**
the singing.
Opera singers have powerful voices.
Their songs tell stories.
Costumes and scenery help to tell the stories.
Often, operas present strong feelings,
such as anger, sadness, or joy.

Farkle Fact

In 1955, Marian Anderson became the first African-American woman to perform at the Metropolitan Opera in New York City. A famous conductor said that she had a voice "that comes once in a hundred years."

Gospel

Gospel is religious music
that is full of energy.
It grew up in America
from African-American folk, blues,
and church songs.
Gospel music is usually sung by a **choir**
at a church service.
The rich, uplifting songs have a lively beat.
Choir members clap or play the tambourine
as they sing.
A piano, organ, or electric guitar often
accompany gospel music.

Farkle Fact

One of the most famous gospel singers in the world was
Mahalia Jackson. She was known as "The Gospel Queen."

Ragtime

Ragtime also began in America.
It was popular in the late 1800s
and early 1900s.
Ragtime music mixes different kinds of rhythms.
It is usually played on the piano
or by a small **band**.
The melodies of ragtime are easy to remember,
but the fast-paced music can be hard to play.
The famous song "Maple Leaf Rag" made
ragtime music popular.
It was written by Scott Joplin.
He was one of the first composers to publish
ragtime music.

Farkle Fact

The word *ragtime* is short for "ragged time." This
describes the different beats and rhythms that
ragtime music uses.

Jazz

Jazz started in New Orleans,
Louisiana.
The first jazz music
was called *Dixieland*.
It grew from African-American folk songs,
ragtime, and the blues.
But jazz added different kinds of rhythms
to this music.
Some jazz music is sung.
Some features instruments only.
Jazz bands feature drums, guitars, pianos,
saxophones, clarinets, and trumpets.
One kind of jazz is **swing**.
It was popular in the 1930s and 1940s.

Farkle Fact

Jazz musicians do something special when they play or sing. They **improvise**. That means that they make up the music as they go along.

15

Marching Music

Marching music has been around
for a long time.
Marching bands play loud,
rhythmic marches.
Marches are designed to accompany
the rhythm of people marching.
John Philip Sousa is the most famous
composer of marches.
You may know his lively march
"The Stars and Stripes Forever."
It features trilling piccolos and crashing cymbals.

Farkle Fact

John Philip Sousa was so well known for his marches
that he was called "The March King."

The Blues

Blues songs began as "field hollers."
These were calls that African-American
plantation workers sang to each other
while they worked in the fields.
Blues music suggests feelings of sadness and pain.
The songs have a special pattern.
The second line of a blues song repeats the first.
The third line is an answer to the first two lines.
Blues music features the guitar and the piano.
Long, slow chords played on the harmonica
are often part of blues music, too.

Farkle Fact

In the 1920s, Bessie Smith became a famous blues singer.
She was nicknamed "Empress of the Blues."

Folk Music

Many cultures around the world
have folk music.
Folk music tells about people
and their history.
Some folk songs are **ballads**
that tell stories and legends.
Most folk songs are not written down.
They are passed along through families and friends,
who play and sing together.
Folk songs often change as they pass
from person to person.
Some folk instruments include the guitar, banjo,
dulcimer, harmonica, and violin.

Farkle Fact

Woody Guthrie was a famous American folk singer
of the 1940s and 1950s. He wrote over 1,000 folk songs
and traveled across the country, sharing his music
about America and its people.

Country and Western

Country and western music
began in the southern part
of the United States in the 1800s.
The **lyrics**, or words, are the most important
part of country songs.
Country singers try to sing very clearly, so listeners
will understand the emotions behind their words.
The simple songs tell stories about people's lives.
The songs might be about love, work, religion,
or the problems that people face.
Country and western music features stringed
instruments, such as the guitar, fiddle, banjo,
and mandolin.

Farkle Fact

Country singer Hank Williams taught himself to play
the guitar when he was only eight years old. His songs
helped country music become well-known all over
the United States during the 1950s.

Rock and Roll

The 1950s brought a new kind
of pop music.
It was called rock and roll.
Rock and roll began as a mix of country
and western music and the blues.
It featured loud electric guitars, heavy
drumbeats, and fast rhythms.
Chuck Berry, Little Richard, and Fats Domino
were some of the first rock stars.
Groups from England, like the Beatles and the
Rolling Stones, helped to make rock and roll
what it is today.

Farkle Fact

Many people think that Elvis Presley was rock music's
greatest star. In the 1950s and 60s, Elvis had numerous
hit songs and starred in over 30 movies. He died in
1977 and is still a beloved rock-and-roll legend today.

Pop Music

Pop music is music that appeals
to a large audience.
The word *pop* is short for "popular."
Jazz, country and western, rap,
and rock and roll are all different types of pop music.
Popular music changes with time
and with what is going on in the world.
When radio was invented, many people could
listen to popular music.
Later, pop music was recorded on records,
cassette tapes, and CDs.
Today, we can even listen to this music
on the computer!

Farkle Fact

Some musicians begin their careers in a certain type
of music, but then switch over to pop music. These
musicians are called *crossover artists*. LeeAnn Rimes is
a popular singer who started her career in country
and western music.

Rap

Rap is a type of pop music.
A rap singer often speaks the words
to a song instead of singing them.
Rhythm instruments play in the background.
Rap music began in New York City
in a neighborhood called the *South Bronx*.
Rap music started when **deejays** talked into
their microphones as they played records.
Rap songs often include **samples**.
Samples are parts of other songs
that are mixed with rap songs.
Rap songs also include music made by
computers and drum machines.

Farkle Fact

In 1979, the Sugar Hill Gang recorded the first popular rap song. It was called "Rapper's Delight" and it sold over 8 million copies.

Vocabulary

accompany–to play music that goes along with singing or dancing. *The orchestra will accompany the singer's solo.*

ballad–a type of song that tells a story. *The ballad was about a girl who lived in Ireland.*

band–a group of musicians who play their instruments together. *The school band practices three times a week.*

choir–a group of people who sing together. *Mom sings in the choir at church.*

composer–a person who writes music. *The composer wrote many popular songs.*

deejay–a person who presents and comments on popular music. *The deejay introduced the new rock-and-roll song to the audience.*

improvise–to make up music while playing it. *We are never sure what song he will play because he likes to improvise his music.*

lyrics–the words to a song. *Bob Dylan writes both the music and the lyrics for his songs.*

minstrel–a musician or entertainer who travels from place to place. *The minstrel juggled balls while he sang.*

orchestra–a group of musicians with sections of string, brass, woodwind, and percussion players. *The orchestra played the music for the ballet.*

samples–parts of a song that are put into another song, usually by means of a computer. *The rap song featured samples of an old pop song.*

swing–a type of dance music of the 1930s, similar to jazz. *The Big Band played swing music while the people danced.*

Think About It!

1. Who was known as "The Gospel Queen"?

2. What kind of instruments do folk musicians usually play?

3. Where did jazz begin?

4. Describe rap music. How is it different from other kinds of music?

5. What is an opera?

The Story and You!

1. What kind of music do you like to listen to? Is it the same kind of music that your parents like?

2. Do you know any country and western singers? Who are they?

3. Do you think that you would enjoy listening to blues music? Why or why not?

4. Which pop stars do you listen to today?

5. If you could be any kind of musician, what kind of music would you like to perform?